Baby animals in grassland habitats

Bobbie Kalman

🌳 Crabtree Publishing Company

www.crabtreebooks.com

The Habitats of Baby Animals

Created by Bobbie Kalman

Dedicated by Crystal Sikkens
For my new nephew, Trent Theodore Kemper

**Author and
Editor-in-Chief**
Bobbie Kalman

Editors
Kathy Middleton
Crystal Sikkens

Design
Bobbie Kalman
Katherine Berti
Samantha Crabtree
(front cover)

Photo research
Bobbie Kalman

Print and production coordinator
Katherine Berti

Prepress technician
Katherine Berti

Illustrations
Jeannette McNaughton-Julich: pages 13, 24 (top right)

Photographs
Corbis: page 12 (bottom)
Corel: pages 1 (middle), 10 (top right), 21 (bottom)
Eyewire: pages 17 (right), 21 (top)
iStockphoto: pages 9, 11 (bottom right), 16 (top), 17 (left)
Photos.com: pages 18 (bottom), 24 (bottom left)
Wikipedia: Adamantios: page 11 (middle right)
Other photographs by Shutterstock

Library and Archives Canada Cataloguing in Publication

Kalman, Bobbie, 1947-
    Baby animals in grassland habitats / Bobbie Kalman.

(The habitats of baby animals)
Includes index.
Issued also in electronic format.
ISBN 978-0-7787-7727-4 (bound).--ISBN 978-0-7787-7740-3 (pbk.)

    1. Grassland animals--Infancy--Juvenile literature. 2. Grassland
ecology--Juvenile literature. I. Title. II. Series: Kalman, Bobbie,
1947- . Habitats of baby animals.

QL115.3.K34 2011   j591.3'909153   C2010-907518-8

Library of Congress Cataloging-in-Publication Data

Kalman, Bobbie.
  Baby animals in grassland habitats / Bobbie Kalman.
      p. cm. -- (The habitats of baby animals)
  Includes index.
  ISBN 978-0-7787-7740-3 (pbk. : alk. paper) -- ISBN 978-0-7787-7727-4
(reinforced library binding : alk. paper) -- ISBN 978-1-4271-9602-6
(electronic (pdf))
  1. Grassland animals--Infancy--Juvenile literature. 2. Grassland animals--
Ecology--Juvenile literature. I. Title.
  QL115.3.K35 2011
  591.74--dc22

                          2010047746

Crabtree Publishing Company

Printed in China/022011/RG20101116

www.crabtreebooks.com   1-800-387-7650
Copyright © **2011 CRABTREE PUBLISHING COMPANY.** All rights reserved. No part of this publication may be reproduced, stored in a retrieval system or be transmitted in any form or by any means, electronic, mechanical, photocopying, recording, or otherwise, without the prior written permission of Crabtree Publishing Company. In Canada: We acknowledge the financial support of the Government of Canada through the Canada Book Fund for our publishing activities.

Published in Canada
Crabtree Publishing
616 Welland Ave.
St. Catharines, Ontario
L2M 5V6

Published in the United States
Crabtree Publishing
PMB 59051
350 Fifth Avenue, 59th Floor
New York, New York 10118

Published in the United Kingdom
Crabtree Publishing
Maritime House
Basin Road North, Hove
BN41 1WR

Published in Australia
Crabtree Publishing
386 Mt. Alexander Rd.
Ascot Vale (Melbourne)
VIC 3032

What is in this book?

What is a habitat?

A **habitat** is a place in nature. Plants and animals live in habitats. They are **living things**. Living things grow, change, and make new living things. Plants make new plants, and animals make babies, like this baby prairie dog. Name two kinds of living things in this picture.

prairie dogs

grass

Living and non-living

Habitats are made up of living and **non-living things**. Air, sunshine, rocks, soil, and water are non-living things. Living things need non-living things. They also need other living things, such as plants and animals. Living things find the things they need in their habitats. Name one non-living thing in this picture that you can see and two that you cannot see but are there.

soil

5

What are grasslands?

Grasslands are mostly flat lands where grasses and other small plants grow. Some grasslands also have a few trees. There are two main kinds of grasslands. They are **temperate grasslands** and **savannas**.

These elephant calves and their mothers live on a savanna in Africa.

Savanna grasslands

Savannas are large grasslands in areas where the weather is warm all year. There are savannas in Africa. Savannas have only two seasons—a **wet season** and a **dry season**. Big animals such as elephants, giraffes, and hippos live on savannas. Lions, cheetahs, and leopards also live there.

Cheetahs are the fastest animals on land. This cheetah cub is already a fast runner.

Prairie grasslands

Temperate grasslands grow in areas with four seasons: spring, summer, autumn, and winter. **Prairies** are temperate grasslands found in Canada, the United States, and Mexico. Prairies can have short or long grasses and flowers but very few trees.

This mule deer mother and her fawn are walking through prairie grasses. The grasses on some prairies are very long.

This coyote pup will soon start hunting rabbits and other small prairie animals with its mother.

Prairie babies

These are just a few of the baby animals that live on prairies. They are baby kit foxes, prairie dog pups, coyote pups, cougar cubs, bison calves, owlets, mule deer fawns, bobcat kittens, ferret kits, and bunnies.

ferret kit

baby kit fox

cougar cub

bunny

bobcat kitten

prairie dog pup

mule deer fawn

bison calf

burrowing owlet

coyote pup

11

Grassland homes

It is not easy for animals to hide on the flat lands of prairies. Many animals dig underground homes so they can keep their babies safe from **predators**. Predators are animals that hunt and eat other animals.

Ferrets live in underground homes.

owlet

owlet

burrow

mother owl

owlet

*Burrowing owls live under the ground in **burrows**, or holes. They do not dig the burrows themselves. They move into homes that badgers or prairie dogs have left. This owl mother has three owlets. The owlets do not have their adult feathers yet.*

12

A prairie dog town

Prairie dogs dig long tunnels under the ground. The tunnels connect rooms. Prairie dogs eat and store food in some rooms and sleep in others. Prairie dog pups stay in rooms called **nurseries**. Prairie dog homes are called **towns**.

entrance

room

nursery

tunnel

The towns stay warm during the cold winter months.

What is a community?

A prairie dog town is a **community**. A community is a place. It is also the group of living things that shares that place. Prairie dogs share their home, food, and jobs. Prairie dog jobs include finding food, babysitting, teaching the pups, guarding the town, and digging tunnels. Meet the prairie dogs and their pups in this amazing community!

Prairie dogs are animals called **mammals**. *They are also* **rodents**. *Rodents are mammals with four front teeth that never stop growing.*

Mammal mothers look after their babies for a long time. Learn more about mammal mothers and babies on pages 16–17.

Prairie dog pups do not come above ground until they are five weeks old. This pup is coming up for the first time.

These young pups are sharing food. Soon, they will go out to look for food with the adults in the town.

Prairie dogs take turns guarding the town. This pup is learning how to spot predators such as coyotes.

Prairie dogs are very friendly with one another. They do group hugs and "kiss" one another when they meet.

Mammal mothers

Mammals are animals with hair or fur. They are born live. After the babies are born, mammal mothers feed them milk from their bodies. Drinking mother's milk is called **nursing**. The coyote pups below are nursing. Most mammal mothers keep their babies safe and teach them how to hunt or find food.

These coyote pups are drinking their mother's milk. Soon, the mother will teach them how to hunt.

Before a coyote baby starts to hunt, it eats meat from its mother's stomach. The mother brings up this food into her mouth. The pup licks its mother's mouth to let her know it is hungry.

After a mule deer fawn is born, its mother hides it in the tall grasses of the prairie. She comes to feed it often. The fawn also starts eating grasses, flowers, and other plants.

Eating plants

Many prairie animals feed on the plants that grow in prairie fields. Animals that feed mainly on plants are called **herbivores**. Rabbits, deer, prairie dogs, and bison are herbivores. They eat the grasses, flowers, and weeds on the prairies. Prairies are also full of insects, such as butterflies and grasshoppers, which feed on plants.

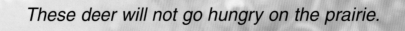

These deer will not go hungry on the prairie.

This bunny rabbit will eat some flowers for lunch.

This bison and her calves have eaten a lot of grass. They came to drink water at a **stream**, or small river.

Prairie carnivores

Carnivores are animals that eat other animals. Prairies have many herbivores, so there are plenty of animals for carnivores to hunt and eat. Red foxes, kit foxes, coyotes, cougars, badgers, owls, falcons, and wolves are just a few of the carnivores that live on prairies.

This young prairie falcon is waiting for its father to bring it food to eat. The chick lets out loud cries that sound like "kree kree kree...kik kik kik." Could it be hungry?

This cougar is hunting a badger. Both badgers and cougars are carnivores. Badgers eat prairie dogs, and cougars eat badgers.

*Kit foxes are **omnivores**. Omnivores eat other animals, but they also eat plants.*

What is a food chain?

Animals need **energy**, or power. They need energy to breathe, move, grow, and stay alive. They get their energy from eating other living things. A **food chain** is the passing of energy from one living thing to another. When an animal eats a plant and another animal eats that animal, there is a food chain.

A prairie food chain

This food chain is made up of prairie coneflowers, a prairie dog, and a bobcat.

*Plants make their own food from air, water, and sunlight. Making food this way is called **photosynthesis**.*

This coneflower has made its own food. It has some of the sun's energy.

coneflower

bobcat

When the prairie dog eats the coneflower, it gets some of the sun's energy.

prairie dog

When the bobcat eats the prairie dog, the sun's energy is passed along from the flower to the prairie dog and then to the bobcat.

23

Words to know and Index

babies
pages 6, 7, 8, 9, 10–11, 12, 14, 16–17, 19, 20

burrows (homes)
pages 12–13

carnivores
pages 20–21

community (town)
pages 13, 14–15

food
pages 13, 14, 15, 16, 17, 18–23

food chain
pages 22–23

herbivores
pages 18, 20

living things
pages 4–5, 14, 22
(**non-living things**
page 5)

Other index words
grasslands pages 6–7, 8–9
habitats pages 4–5
mammals pages 14, 16, 17
mothers pages 6, 8, 9, 12, 14, 16–17
nursing page 16
omnivores page 21
photosynthesis page 23
plants pages 4, 5, 6, 17, 18–19, 21, 22, 23
prairie dogs pages 4, 10, 11, 12, 13, 14–15, 18, 21